# Heart Work

A Heart-Centered Collection of Poems

Melissa Whiteford St. Clair



First Edition

Book cover design by POWERSTORY
Book jacket design by DJR Designs

# DEDICATION

Honoring five black men whose lives were ended in lynching in Greenville County, SC.

Robert Williams (1881)
Ira Johnson (1895)
Tom Keith (1899)
George Green (1933)
Willie Earle (1947)

# ACKNOWLEDGEMENTS

In gratitude

To Kathy Goughenour, Business Coach and Trainer for Virtual Assistants who invited Lynne Hurdle Price, Conflict Resolution Strategist to speak to our Virtual Expert® Community about diversity, equity, and inclusion.

To Dr. Lynne Maureen Hurdle, Conflict Resolution Strategist for continuing to be my "Conductor" through her courses On The Matter Of Race: White People Committed to Continuing the Journey Together.

To my husband, Matt St. Clair for his support and encouragement.

To my true-blue mentor, Donna Keel Armer, author of "Solo in Salento."

To Dominique Tuttle, Gallery Manager/Curator, Gullah Art Gallery/Museum.

To my sounding board, Perry Jenkins.

To Pat Conroy and his activism against institutional racism and bigotry.

# Introduction

Heart Work A Heart-Centered Collection of Poems is the second of the author's responses to her assignments related to the course On The Matter of Race: White People Committed to Continuing the Journey Together, Level 2 (May 2021-October 2021), Level 3 (January 2022 through June) and Level 4 (September 2022 through publication).

Additional inspiration for the poetry came from participation in a JustFaith Ministries workshop Faith and Racial Equity along with independent study.

The author is grateful for the opportunities, education, and growth sparked by these experiences.

A section of lighthearted poems written while on vacation rounds out this collection.

# Table of Contents

# Heartwork

Heartwork is **your purpose combined with passion;** it is taking whatever your heart has been charged with and committing to do the work necessary to honor your spirit.
(tanayawinder)

# Matters of the Heart

**Bruised**


I am sharing outward.

How I am looking inward.

As I'm on my journey

        to learn more about race.

For a better understanding

of constructs longstanding.


Far from the accusations of race-baiting
and bigotry.

My message is and will be unity.


Strong words against me being used
for expressing my views.

Labels I won't claim but I do admit the
bruise.


Giving myself and others grace

as I continue my course of study On The
Matter Of Race.

## Blue-tailed skink

Blue-tailed skink

A smirk and a wink


Watching the world go by leaning on the
counter of her kitchen sink


The kitchen a hub for her family

Fried chicken and sweet tea were her
specialties.


The whir of the electric mixer mashing
potatoes

A giggle after telling a joke about green
tomatoes


Quick with a quip

The only "dirty" word,

*shit*

would cross those rouged lips

A penny for the thoughts

I'd give to know what she was thinking


Looking past two massive maples

Turning to see the people she cherished
sitting 'round her table


Games played with cards or marbles, or
tiles

Kept living light-hearted despite life's
trials


Friends and family would flock for miles

To stop, porch sit, and reminisce a while.

## Vantage Point

Making a choice
Using my voice

I choose to speak my truth.

The drama to remove
The discord to diffuse

Release the stress accrued
Just the facts, not misconstrued

Take responsibility
To boldly step into "me."

## Wrong Number

My first memory of you
Is a vignette before I was two

A pudgy pug nose girl
With a head of blonde curls

Plopped in an empty Utz potato chip can did
. . . . glide

A snack container along a checkerboard floor
like a carnival ride

You give everyone a nickname
Pooky was mine

Not sure of the origin. You never shared.
I assumed it was special,
that it indicated you cared.

The nickname was given away, you say
Repurposed to another gal in town, one day

In your Contacts two people bear the same name
So it wasn't unique, not mine to claim

Incoming calls from you were always rare

Nowadays a fat-finger misdial and quick
disconnect - the ring unintentional, but caller
ID is still there

Don't butt dial me
Buzz ME by mistake
A lifespan of minimal communication
Makes my heart ache

# Library Voice

I was told by an elementary school teacher to
use my library voice.

So I tried to lower and found I could not
reduce to a murmur or whisper - it didn't seem
to be a choice.

At home, yes, quiet with no sisters or
brothers.

Hollering fanfare at team sports. I could belt
out cheers at pep rallies and such for others.

All appropriate places to be loud.

I made the JV and Varsity squad to hail the
green and gold, so proud.

Through a series of lifetime circumstances, I
was quiet every day.

Self-preservation as an ACOA, then required by
HIPAA, OPSEC, PERSEC, no PDA.

Eventually I became so quiet I lost the urge
for spontaneous speech.

The ability to express myself and ask for what
I want and need.

Once I took heed, I made a choice.

It has taken a lot of effort to work through,
to undo, to allow myself to be heard.

I'm working to be vocal through my writing and
spoken word.

## Day-Old Beer

The flavor of the air stale like a day-old beer
The familial house - Why keep coming back here?

Superficial conversations in fits and starts.
A delicious home-cooked meal dotted with
belches and farts.

Always living away due to hub's career
Gulps of hope chased with fear popping the top
on the obligatory visit year after year

Chilled by memories of pensive waits for
drunken returns
Even with age, my stomach churns

Storming in or in a stupor through an unlocked
kitchen door
Work boots tread, or trip across the floor

Settling into a chair worn by his weight
A shotgun propped behind it in the corner
Heart-racing, wondering what will be our fate?

Change of clothes ready if the room must be
. . . . . fled
Will he settle down and go to bed?

Holding breath, bedroom latch locked
Will we even hear it being cocked?

Tonight, like others he stumbles on into the
bath to wind down docile or heated hyper spurn.
Brushing teeth, last piss before raising a
glass to a new morn.

A term I learned for this experience, ACOA
Will these thoughts of never being enough ever
go away?                 Apparently not today.

## DAR

Daughters of the American Revolution

A one hundred thirty-two-year-old
institution

A service organization for women, but
you gotta be related

To someone who participated

From a patriot you gotta be a descendant

In efforts toward independence


Through efforts of my cousin, Christopher

After a three-year application process,
I'm a DAR card carrier

The patriot? Private John Osborne

In Captain John Rodgers' Company 5

He enlisted September 15, 1775.

Ain't it grand these records we derive?

This privileged status

Obtained by gratis

Weighs heavily

Leaves me cofounded mightily

When not every American can trace

Their ancestors, or even how they got to
this place

Names not written on the U.S. census list

It's by sheer miracle and fortitude, a
population of enslaved people would persist

In 1939, First Lady Eleanor Roosevelt,
her DAR membership resigned

When the performance of world-renowned
singer, Marian Anderson was denied

Why? Because of the color of her skin

Fast-forward to 2004, the DAR welcomed the
first African American woman to its
national governing board.

Ready to lean-in in 2020, the **E Pluribus
Unum Educational Initiative** began

A commitment to research and honor
Revolutionary soldiers, Indigenous and
African

Shared history.

Initiatives to tell a more complete story

**What America Means to Me**


Democracy

Hypocrisy

Boiling points

Melting pot


Juxtaposition

Traditions

Assimilate

Don't congregate

Unity

Impunity


Unrest

Blessed

Dressing graves

Heroes ne'er forgot

## Beaufort National Cemetery

# Clinging Vine

Penny in her shoe

Something borrowed, something blue.


Heart a-flutter in the ready room

About to walk down the aisle to wed her groom.


The advice received as she envisioned hearts entwined,

"No man wants a clinging vine…"


Heartsink for that split second of time.
Tucked away to the back of her mind

As the organ played and the wedding bells chimed.


Little did the soothsayer know

As the spouse of an active-duty Marine

She would live her life predominantly solo

While her grunt answered the call of the DOD's machine.


A demanding gun club that claimed his attention

Moving from duty station to duty station triggered constant reinvention.

Trailing him. She lost herself. She found
herself and lost herself again.

Being hyper-aware of the boxes a military
spouse finds oneself put in.


While he climbed the ranks

She clung to planting roots.


Bloom where you're planted,

A quote for living the military spouse
lifestyle often used.


Many a holiday, anniversary, birthday spent
alone.

Waiting for mail or a call from an overseas sat
phone.


The September birthday flower, a morning glory

The flowers are resilient with the ability to
grow through adversity.

Traits to help her meander through her journey.


Vines coil, twist, and bend

        Making concessions

    Altering directions

Weaving a circle of support, a network of
friends.

Just being yourself was finally a truth she
realized near his career's end.

# A Vicious Disguise

Before a date
In the living room we did wait

Nervous teens
Me, always nervous in knots in your
presence, it seemed

You appeared in a white robe
A vicious disguise.
Your authority to legitimize?
Positioned, standing with leering eyes.

A family heirloom pulled from the cedar
chest
From a white supremacist past
Made from rough cotton, a fabric woven to
last.
A uniform emblazoned with a circular crest.
The pointed tip of the mask askew
The attire too small for you at six foot
two.
In the right hand carryeth your favorite
brew.

Tied tight 'round your growing beer gut by
a cord tassel
The original owner, an uncle, wore this
guise to hassle.

Did you wear it to appear as a member of
the Klan
To gain an upper hand
On matters of race we white teens didn't
understand?

Now I do better understand the matters of
race.
No respect for the man who thinks terror is
funny by hiding his face.

Wearing this cloak
For what purpose?
To conjure a joke.
Fear, fright, and horror it did invoke.

Mimicking your long-dead uncle?
You stood there and chuckled

A lasting impression wearing that garment
of hate.
Along with your put-downs, your insults,
and other ploys to berate.

Fight or flight
Wrong versus right
Thoughts in my head
Hurt in my heart
Your actions further tearing our daddy-
daughter relationship apart.

The shock that day
My conscience trying to explain.

Learning what systemic racism has been
through history,
HIS story,
YOUR story,
MY story.

No voice.
Now a voice
Speaking up.
Speaking out.

## Surrender

On a gorgeous day in the foothills of the
Blue Ridge mountains

In her hands she held pieces of paper and
little stones.

Green Aventurine.
A clearer of the heart space.
Encouraging one to find courage, strength,
and grace.

Surrender was the word she chose for me.

I did not understand the context
immediately.

Busy living life fully.

Stopped in my tracks two days later by an
injury.

I lunged too far and landed hard.
Stretched and jarred.

Muscle striations, reverberations.
Followed by . . .
Rest. Ice. Compression. Elevation.

Slowed to a snail's pace.
My new mantra, "the turtle wins the race."

Surrender was the word she chose for me.
I now understand it was a foreshadow for
humility.

Surrendering to a myriad of feelings.
Surrendering to time for healing.

## The Widow

The morning cough sounded like smoked
cigarettes

She had a bad taste in her mouth

A mixture of gin and bile


Today was going to be a bad day, she said


Her mind was wandering into places of guilt
and shame

Her husband's death, herself she did blame.

The coffee was black, the newspaper was
read.

Over and over "oh my," she said

Time fading the mind, weakening the soul,
and wearing on the heart

The vows spoken so long ago, til death do
us part

## Child's Play


Kids left alone to their own devices
Parents took off to indulge their vices.


After games of tag and hide-n-seek
Boredom loomed
Was the afternoon doomed?


The only boy you went to the primary
bedroom closet
Bewilderment as to what would cause it


You brought out the shotgun
A real gun, a weapon
My daddy said never point a gun at anyone.


Fun and games ceased
Was this game one where we call the police?


Fight or flight took over
Wanting to run, we froze in place
Color draining, hearts pounding full pace

Was it loaded?

No one knows

Minutes passed by, and more fear arose.


Could there be a trigger puller behind that
baby fuzz face?


Scared

Unprepared

Victims in a lair?


Shotgun pointed; the boy glared


Okay now this isn't fun.
Put down the gun.


We all crept back to the living room, room
for the living but remained stunned.

On that day innocence won.

## Mallory Beach

Missing from a boat accident on Archers
Creek.

Answers to so many questions the public
still seeks.


Without warning

In the wee hours of a February morning


Striking pilings by a concrete bridge
The impact must have been
Like a wrecking ball
Crashing against an immovable wall


Sending boat contents and bodies flying
The responsible party in perpetuity denying


Your name called in a cacophony of southern
drawls
First responders and other representatives
of law


The Beaufort Gazette newspaper read,
"Mallory Beach hit her head."

We lived aboard Parris Island
and drove by your search party for days.

A never-ending line of cars and boaters
looking for you in the waterway.


Bearing witness to misery of a daily search
party

Would you be found lifeless or with just a
few scars?

Searchers suffering anguish and pain as
they tried to deal with the looming reality


Law enforcement scoured the causeway

To determine the way to the cause


You floated just beyond reach, bobbing
under brackish water toward the Broad

Veering by darting fish
Drifting in the water like driftwood


Five miles in total through sun and moon

High and low tides

Days passed; hope loomed
Your fate all must abide


The Beaufort Gazette newspaper read,
"Mallory Beach found dead."


Seven days later to be found, drowned,
by a boat launch.

After the boat you were on launched you
into memories that haunt.


Leaving family and friends and the
community mourning.

Memories of you enduring.


Rest in peace in mystery, in memories,
Mallory Beach.

## White Rabbit

She hopped up from a TV show that had a
white rabbit
Was it about a 70s leftover psychedelic
drug habit?

Teenage tinsel teeth
Astride a shiny new 10-speed

Beaming with pride
An early birthday present
    from her grandmother to ride

Pedaling fast in a short set and tennies
on the hot asphalt.

Steering her two wheel,
shifting then to coast...
Toward the driveway marked by the wagon
wheel post.

Listening over her shoulder to turn left.
Looking once,
twice
but not three times.

Perhaps a rabbit's foot,
or third glance
would've been a charm.

To sound the alarm,
to realize the impending harm.

Turn, bang, crunching metal, car, bike, and
bones.

Windshield cracking when met by the back of
her head.

Tumbling, tumbling like a somersault,
Rolling in the air.

Quiet like a dream, lacking reality,
drifting like that hare.

No sound just hazy warmth, is she alive or
dead?

Back at home, the doe hears the police
scanner blare, "a bicycle rider had been
struck."

Her father, a farmer, heard the crash and
ran with the dog from his pick-up truck.

On her back in the ditch, knees up.

Fuzzy headed and not focusing on the late
summer sky
Like other days lying on her back in the
grass creating animals from clouds passing
by.

Her mind trying to unravel
why her skin was pinching from lying on
gravel.


She crept back to consciousness near the
mailbox large enough to stuff a month's
worth of mail.
Father there, now panting from the sprint,
dog pacing, wagging his tail.

The ambulance screamed.

She'd just ridden that new bike to go see
her Meem.


Onto the backboard,
a neck brace encircling,
legs covered with inflated devices.


Into the emergency vehicle speeding over
the state line.


Her first near-death experience
But it wasn't her time.


The driver and his daughter,
stunned and shocked sitting in a white VW
rabbit.


Ripples of trauma affecting all. It was an
accident.


The bike was too new to be given a name.
That third sprint could have been grave.


In the chicken house for years remained
A twisted, bent bike frame.


Saved by her father. Why was it there?
To remind **him** of the sobering scare?


Or a cooped-up reminder it was
**Her** own ass-fault.

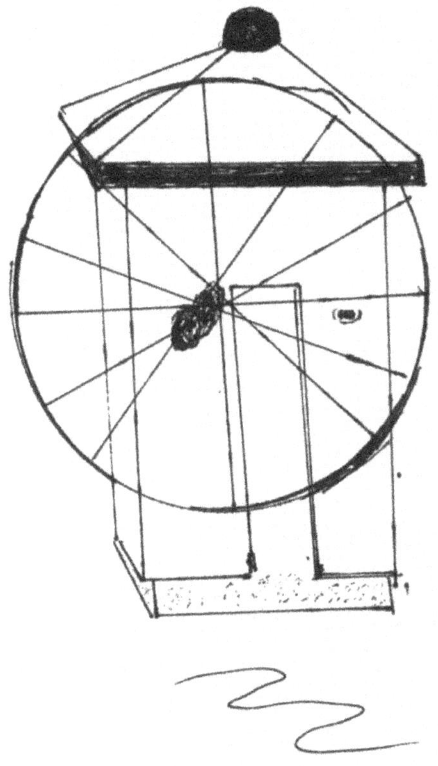

Pen & Ink: Janet M. Whiteford

## Roots

A farm on a hill
Established long ago

Turning over sod
Deep down in my soul

Furrow lines across my brow
Growing questions my mind does plow

Timber and stone farmhouse
History playing cat and mouse

Whitewashed workshop, shed and barn
House equipment, fodder, and animal scarn

Fertile fields
Agriculture crops did yield

Across the state line another farm resides
A carpenter, his wife and four children did
preside

Woodshop filled with tools to build
Agrarian acres to be tilled

Honoring past in the present
All sides of the story, my roots represent

# Voices

Voices
Choices
Scrolling through my mind
Keeping me awake
Some brutal
Some kind

Tossing, turning
Counting numbered sheep
Lists left undone
Doubts and fears my reasoning can't outrun

Restless
Breathless
Eyes wide open
Or pinched shut

Inhale
Exhale
Ruminating rut

Deliberate
Wanton
Out of my control

Next, please
People-please
Self-talk turning 'round

Exhausted
Voices quieted
Finally, sleeping sound

**Memory**


My first memory is of a black and white
checkerboard floor
Where I played games
While my mom chopped vegetables on a
cutting board

Crawling into the living room
Past the 1960s TV set
I remember the scratch of the earthy multi-
color shag carpet

In a neat, little grey house
Narrow, like a stovepipe
This is where I spent the first two years
of my life.

# Inkling

Skin tingling with goosebumps
Hairs standing on end

Who's around the corner?

An enemy, a close friend

Perhaps one and the same
Buried guilt, harboring shame

Skin tingling with goosebumps
Hairs standing on end

What's around the corner?

A new beginning, a bitter end

Looking down, looking up
Empty glass, full cup

Where will we be
When we see
A "Beloved Community"
Or will it remain only a dream, an inkling?

# Lighthearted

## A Kiskadee

A kiskadee came to breakfast.
"A table for two, please."

For the rooster, a coffee
For the hen, a cuppa tea

The kiskadee ordered European Style Muesli
The missus ordered oatmeal with Bermuda
Honey

A sparrow came to say hello
"Chirp, chirp" peeped the jolly fellow

The palm fronds swayed to and fro
As the kiskadee pondered, where will this
day go?

## A Sparrow

A sparrow came to dinner

Before the drinks were served

He perched on the corner of the table

Such a good-humored bird

We exchanged pleasantries

Twittered a few words

Then he was ready to go

Though just before he flew off,

he puffed UP

          and left a download.

**A Longtail**

A Longtail came to lunch
He brought a few friends, making it a bunch

They told a sordid tale
About a ship that sailed

Filled with grindstones bound for Baltimore
Maryland
The ship sank meeting its end

The crew was saved
Using the stones, the yard was paved

Finishing their story
The Longtails departed in a flurry

## Precious Resource

A precious resource
From the heavens

Delicious clear drops
Cascade toward the earth

Onto white painted roofs
With horizontal grooves

Designed to catch rain
Trickles into a cistern

Waiting to be tapped
Clean water, life to sustain

# On The Matter of Race

# Complex History

Unpacking a complex history
So much untold remains a mystery

Systemic, not singular isolated incidents
Divisive systems put into place by past
presidents

Men of their time they say, you see
Using free labor, chattel slavery

White ancestors may have been poor
They freely came to these shores

A better life to explore

Indentured, maybe

Those terms had an end date
Opportunity, not being property was their
fate

White people have had it hard
But never had to fear awakening to a
burning cross in their yard

People polarized
People of color oppressed and ostracized

Take a moment to look back with me

Improving quality of life for others
Is improving quality of life for all
humanity

## White Supremacy

White Supremacy
A belief of white superiority

What persona do you see?
A skinhead with tats, a symbol of Nazi?

The reality can also be
A white face that is you or me.

A white chaos creator in a Capitol riot
A sea of white faces
Violating off-limits spaces
But nary a shot in defense fired.

Suppressive systems set up throughout
history
To many of us are still a mystery
The technicolor version of reality not ours
to see

I want to learn the full peacock
Not the founding father's version they spun
to preserve their stock
The full spectrum of stories yet to unlock

On a journey to gain a deep perspective
I've become a history detective
It's no longer elective
But a calling, a directive.

## Statuary

Unity is more important to me
Than a manmade piece of statuary

Erected on phallic pedestals
For too many decades cruel spectacles

Visual obstacles
To a landscape more equitable

The Virginia Supreme Court says,
"a democracy values change."
"Public policies change."

Too bad systems transformation
can't happen faster.
As removing a hunk of plaster.

**Taking a Knee**

Taking a knee
A plea

A quiet gesture for the world to see

Speaking volumes, a call for social justice
and unity

Met with scrutiny

To you it seems unclear

An action to jeopardize a dream, a career

In response to continued cries of ancestors
from yesteryear

From this humble position
League leaders began to listen

A reverb of sorts
Throughout pro sports

## Nice White Lady

I'm a nice white lady, no lie

I ain't being shady -

I'll even tell you the color of my hair
dye.


Now and then, there is a gal,

a nice white lady cloaked in gray

Don't piss her off or look at her the wrong
way.


She'll create a storyline beyond rationale


She'll wield her white privilege

Reconstruct everything that was said


Reverse the verse

To make matters worse

An encounter fueled with hatred.

The receiver filled with dread,
praying there won't be any bloodshed.


A "Karen" in a bombastic display

An irate spectacle with something caustic
to say


Part of her act

Is misconstruing the facts


There are bad apples you see

Sowing seeds laced with white fragility


That white face might as well be behind a
mask from the past


But this is the present and people harbor
hate, ill will and discontent

Their white supremacy at the ready to
represent.


Watch your back. I'm watching it too.
Trying to make a difference with the words
I use.

## Engine

Can you imagine

Always being conscious of the color of your
skin

Constantly guarded, on the surface and
within


Super successful

Confident, talented, admired

Yet hypervigilant, guarded and stress-full


While speaking meek and mild, tired

When telling of experiencing racism as a
child.


Despite all the points scored, millions of
audience roars

The history of these facts spoken cannot be
ignored.


The sting of the knowledge a slaver hurled
a weight at a small child

Hitting Araminta Ross in the head, instead

From slavery she eventually fled

Those systemic engines still burning

While society learning

The situation should be concerning

A more equitable world yearning

For systems change churning

Gears toward equity turning

Instead of by (white) people, for (white) people

This can't be the way it's always going to be


Take a minute to learn about your fellow man

There is opportunity for all in this promised land

Listen.

Learn.

Believe.

Understand.

A better world for all is our hands.

# White Washing

Whitewashing, of Thee I sing

Of history, let ignorance ring

The educational system failed
to school you and me

Perpetuating illiteracy of U.S. history

That hurts my heart and numbs my psyche


Preserving a white-washed story for
knowledge seeking minds

Full knowledge hiding - in white-washed
pages it's confined

A picture painted by the founding father's
design

Hidden figures, harsh reality

Chalk it up to white fragility


Truth like fingernails across the
blackboard

Screaming to be put on the record


Tree of knowledge

Don't take a bite

An apple for teacher

Dotting I's and crossing T's with a #2 yellow graphite


Curriculums avoiding

Ignoring, rather than exploring

Around history skirting

Truth averting

Responsibility shirking

Danger flirting

Further division lurking

I find this disconcerting.


Without truth from the past, we risk reverting

Without lessons learned, we risk propagating

The status quo - because we don't know what we don't know

Wearing rose-colored glasses causing learners to be blind

I'm studying, learning, writing, and speaking these rhymes

**Policies**

Take a walk with me

Through US history

Where a timeline of policies

Established, reinforced, coerced
inequities.


The Racial Wealth Gap

Long term effects, lifetimes of unjust
systems to unpack.


Hours after his honorable discharge

South Carolina police pulverized

Sgt Isaac Woodard's eyes

The offense? Wearing a United States Army
uniform while being black

A decorated veteran.

The incident led to desegregation actions
by President Harry Truman


I'm getting ahead of myself – time hopping

Let's go back to 1865 and Andrew Jackson's
Land Policies and Sharecropping

40 acres and a mule

Freedom fuel


For recently freed enslaved who fought in
the Civil War

Rescinded

Serving their country, now serving their
former masters once more.


Black farmers subjected to land seizures
and imposed eminent domain

Displaced, without rights to reclaim, their
livelihoods forever changed.


Ready for some more?

Let's move onto the National Housing Acts
of 1934.

Maps were made, given a red shade

Given a "D" grade

The ability of black home ownership did
degrade


In 1935, the Social Security Act

Intended a safety net for workers, unless
you were black

Omitting workers, domestic and on the farm

An unemployment rate 80% higher for blacks
than whites did the harm


The Fair Labor Standards Act of 1938

Excluded tip-based occupations employing
black workers struggling to earn a wage


Now we come to 1944, the G.I. Bill

Government issue, it turns my GI system
inside out

World War II heroes of color denied
benefits

On a high post Jim Crow sits


"Separate but Equal," not a new theme, a
historical sequel.

Segregated schools, housing, jobs, and
swimming pools.


The glaring reality of white privileges.

The bravery of six-year-old Ruby Bridges.

Full details of history omitted in school.

Lack of this knowledge today, keeping us
fools.

Bell-bottoms and disco dancing on a parquet floor

To get lost in funky music of the 1970's, sublime.

Mortgage lenders steering black homeowners to loans, subprime


The 1971 War on Drugs

Profiling black people as addicts and thugs

Incarceration, the answer for breaking the law

Implementing employment restrictions, further deepening the fall


A criminal record, collateral consequences

Instead of second chances, the government builds more cages and fences.


Deep-seated racial inequity

Across the centuries

Taking on these issues with poetry

Will I live to see

Jesus' final prayer, "make them one," a reality.

**PERVASIVE**

Persuasive in its pitch

Pervasive, so most think in history it's
only a stich [in time]

A long-lasting influence

To maintain white affluence

Don't question it or you're being a
nuisance

It's modern-day impact under constant
issuance

Its tentacles twine through systems

As deep as sugar cane is high,

As deep as a rice field ditch,

As deep as an indigo vat,

As sharp as a cotton blade.

Quick as a whip to keep "others" in their
place.


The human body

A commodity

To build with heavy labor, the economy

Years, fears, tears, keeping "others" in arrears.

No mercy, just PTSD

No fair trial, no clemency

Only denial, for centuries

Over time, and even today –

Some promises made then swept away


With open mind, open heart, open eyes, open ears

To read, to feel, to see, to listen and to hear

How racism continues to invade

Slow progress toward equity

Because of preclusions, presumptions, assumptions around skin shade.

## At the Corner of Lynch and Main


Did you see the police officer with his knee on the neck

Of George Floyd and hear his cries as he was drained of his last breath?


Arrested then killed in broad daylight

While a crowd of people witnessed his plight


No jail

No bail

Another legal system fail


For passing a fake $20 bill

To the convenience store Till


Did that give the right to kill before trial

A scenario on repeat, so vile


But law enforcement's duty is to serve and protect

I protest!

At the corner of Lynch and Main

Not an angry white mob but a lone gunman looking to kill and maim

A white supremacist plotted, planned, and then took aim


After selecting a grocery store in a black neighborhood

At 18 years old, racist hatred so deep, at the onset of adulthood


When will it be enough bodies, black and brown?

To spur leaders and lay people to decry and denounce?


At the corner of Lynch and Main


Over 400 years have passed, yet cycles of hatred and unjust systems remain

Yes, history is to blame.


Brought on by laws of the forefathers to control the population

Imbalance of restrictions and rights to force division and segregation

Barriers to harmony need to be
acknowledged, reframed.

Let us not let hate win and leave life to
this continuous kill game.


Longstanding discord and racism devastate
society

All in support of white supremacist
propriety.

**Proof**

You say it's black and white
No, I say, that can't be right.
Can't be anything but a shade of gray.

But here's the proof,
My credentials
So put your doubt away.

Why the need for me to defend
As you fail to comprehend?

Why am I on trial
Because of your default of denial?

Bias and distrust
Prejudices always at play

Tugging, twisting
When we should be actively listening

Not second guessing
Questioning

Can it really be "x?"
The broader query is "why?"

Take my word for face value
No need to read between the lines

The proof is in my experience. Believe me
when I tell you the first time.

## The Rope Burns

God created me for good
To live a long, full life

From seed, to sprout, to seedling, to
sapling
Rooted in solid ground, firmly standing

Growing strong and tall
Refuge for His creatures, big and small

A bird's nest on my shoulder
A squirrel tucked into a knot

Giving oxygen, and shade, never taking away

Mighty with dignity

I would never have known from my infancy
I would be a lynching tree

A mob rushes
The forest hushes

Footfall makes my sap turn cold
White supremacy, Jim Crow, so bold

Weak men leveraging my strength
Hatred so vile makes my leaves shake

The rope burns as it twists and turns
A life taken; no lessons learned

When they cut him down, they dragged his
body away.
For a bolt of lightning to strike me down,
I did pray.

My appeal for forgiveness came in the form
of a dove
Peace be with you was the message raining
down from Above

Bound by silence while my scarred bark
decays
Only the dismantling of systemic racism,
the injustice can assuage

I extend an olive branch to humanity
For my role as an accessory to this
calamity

# Customs House

Bustling, busy people walking to and fro
Wood floors creaking from the heavy foot
flow

Stepping over or on a peacock feather-like
mark
Or catching a boot toe on a hand-hewn nail
distracted by goods being debarked

While seeking, meeting, greeting merchants,
doing business you know

A belly laugh
A frown
A joy
A conversation turned 'round

Did Robert Smalls pause to catch a glimpse
of the creek
As a bead of sweat rolled down his cheek?
A constant trickle in the southern heat.

The churn of government
Deals to foment

The floors trodden
Dry with dust or rain sodden

The platform for oversight of imported or
exported goods.
Still standing with its original brick and
wood.

**STONO**

The heartbeat of a people

They took the drums away


Underneath a steeple

They worshipped anyway


Banding together

Mother Afrika tether


A revolt led by Jemmy

Slaves sought liberty!


Skin whipped with leather

The plans held tight as a feather


Joining together near the Stono River

A rebellion lodged against slaveholding
whites reached the Edisto River


The colonizers looked to their King

The Negro Act of 1740 he did bring

Whites tightened their grip

No assembly, no learning, and drums they
did strip


White control tried to stop the music

No! The tempo kept composing

# Geysers of Gratitude

Lights off, thoughts on

Geysers of gratitude

Keeping me awake

Feelings of triumph

I cannot shake

Vibrations plumb

Emotions hum

Heart pounding

Breath resounding

Joy abounding

Love surrounding

Finding grounding

All the mind-body work to lessen the hurt

Trauma concealing

Pain revealing.

Processing.

Progressing…

Layers peeled away

Allowing the mind to play

Before I close my eyes to pray

And give thanks for the moment to feel this way

# Reference

ACOA – Adult Child of an Alcoholic

HIPAA – Health Insurance Portability and Accountability Act

OPSEC – Operational Security

PERSEC – Personal Security

PDA – Public Display of Affection

# ABOUT THE AUTHOR

Melissa Whiteford St. Clair grew up a stones throw from the Mason-Dixon Line in Whiteford, Maryland. She married her high school sweetheart and for the next 30 years, home was where the U.S. Marine Corps sent them. Putting down roots in South Carolina, she found herself emotionally affected by the rise in social injustice in our country she dedicated herself to learning more about racism. While participating in the course "On The Matter of Race: White People Committed to Beginning the Journey Together," poetry became a processing mechanism for her thoughtful reflections and responses to homework assignments resulting in her first chapbook **Home Work A Collection of Poems Sparked by One White Woman's Journey on the Matter of Race**. A lifelong learner, Melissa's study of matters of race continues along with involvement in antiracism efforts and sharing her words at poetry readings and open mic events.

Beyond writing poetry, Melissa is an entrepreneur and owner of Paper Chaser Biz LLC where she helps busy women solopreneurs free their time by proving professional virtual assistant services. She has an affinity for bees, yoga, and porch sitting.

# SPECIAL THANKS

To my mentor, Patti Bozman for helping me curate this book of work.

To Karley Conklin, writer, and poetry workshop extraordinaire.

To Joan H. Hodous, Artist, Author, Activist, Businesswoman, and Painter, for her appraisal of this book of heartfelt poetry.

All sharing open and honest critique.

# CONNECT ON SOCIAL

www.whitegirladvocacy.com

www.linkedin.com/company/white-girl-advocacy-llc

www.linkin.com/in/melissastclair

www.facebook.com/whitegirladvocacy

www.instagram.com/whitegirladvocacy

www.youtube.com/@whitegirladvocacy/videos

www.whitegirladvocacy.com/book-shelf

# IMAGE ACKNOWLEDGEMENTS

Trey Nelson, SoutherNothings-Unity photos

Learn more about the Unity Mural at https://www.centerforcreativepartnerships.org/projects

Much to the author's dismay, the Unity Mural was whitewashed in December 2022. Read more in her blog: Unity Erased at https://whitegirladvocacy.com/blog/f/unity-erased

Author's personal photos

Pen & Ink by Janet M. Whiteford

# Harriet Tubman Monument

A portion of proceeds from the sale of each book will be donated to **The Harriet Tubman Monument,** Beaufort, SC until monies are raised for installation.

Unity Mural, Beaufort, SC

# Order of Poems

**Matters of the Heart**
Bruised
Blue-tailed Skink
Vantage Point
Wrong Number
Library Voice
Day-Old Beer
DAR
What America Means to Me
Clinging Vine
A Vicious Disguise
Surrender
The Widow
Child's Play
Mallory Beach
White Rabbit
Roots
Voices
Memory
Inkling

**Lighthearted**
A Kiskadee
A Sparrow
A Longtail
Precious Resource

**On the Matter of Race**
Complex History
White Supremacy
Statuary
Taking a Knee
Nice White Lady
Engine
White Washing
Policies
Pervasive
At the Corner of Lynch and Main
Proof
The Rope Burns
Customs House
STONO
Geysers of Gratitude